It is Not a Dot!

Written by Isabel Thomas

Illustrated by Sharon Harmer

It is not a dot!

It is a dog on a mat!

Dip it into the pot!

It is a cat and a mop!

Dot!

Dip!

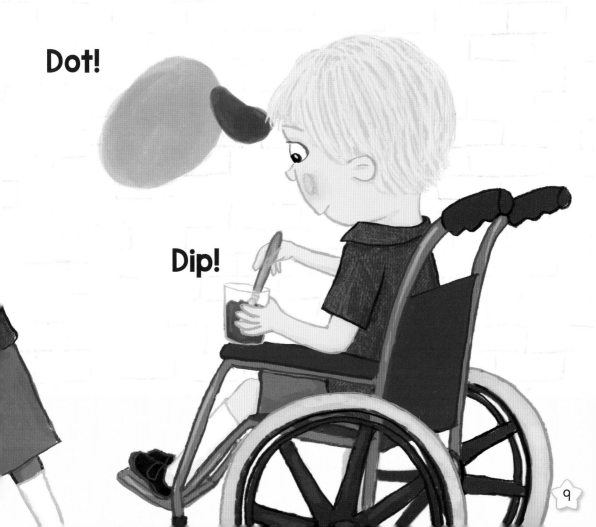

dog

cat

It is a kid in a cap!

kid

Talk about the story

Ask your child these questions:

1 What was painted on the wall at the start of the story?

2 What did the children dip their brushes into?

3 Which three animal names were in the story?

4 How can you tell the children were painting outside?

5 Have you ever seen a painting on a wall? What did it look like?

6 If you had to turn a dot into a picture, what would you draw?

Can your child retell the story in their own words?